Blink

poetry of living and losing

Mandy Whyman

Lavender Button Books

The right of Mandy Whyman to be identified as author of this work has been asserted in accordance with the Copyright, Designs and Patents Act 1988

Copyright © 2025 Mandy Whyman

All rights reserved. This book or any portion thereof may not be reproduced or used in any manner whatsoever without the express written permission of the author.

Cover image: Javardh - Unsplash

"No man ever steps in the same river twice, for it's not the same river and he's not the same man."

Heraclitus

Contents

Blink	9
Shadow	10
String	11
All Words Are Water	12
Into The Ether	14
Hours	15
Stage Four	16
Dark	18
Faith	20
December	22
Journey By Train	23
Lights	24
Tenderness and Tears	26
The Tractor Shed	28
Ballad of the Voter	30

Snow	31
End Game	32
Here I Am	34
Of Love and Mortality	36
Identity	38
Will We Know?	40
Morning	41
Revenge	42
Follower	44
Get Up	46
Time Heals	48
Falling	49
All That We Are	50
Memory	52
The Poets and The Dreamers	53

Letterbox	54
Ghosts	55
This Longing	56
Ordinary Things	58
If We Mine The Moon	59
Waiting	60
Clockwork	61
Solstice	62
New Year's Eve	64
These Words	66

Blink
===

Blink.

The click of the camera shutter,

An instant stilled, stopped.

Blink.

The scene on a moving train

That streaks out in ribboned fields and towns

And lights and suns and days.

The sudden full-stop dark of the tunnel.

Blink.

The world caught stark in a lightning flare.

Blink.

This kiss. This smile. This word.

Eyes wide, hold on – hold!

Like light. Like breath.

Blink.

Shadow

The breath of this mortality

Lies close to the touch:

The sigh of a lover on the nape of the neck;

The soft fall of satin on skin.

This shadow so bound to our being,

Tethered to our footsteps, our tracks.

It echoes in our songs,

Plays games in the whorls of our prints,

Kisses our eyes as we sleep.

We are whole and nothing,

Done and undone all at once

In this brief, this tender blink of dancing

This melancholy: this startling:

This sweet breath of mortality.

String

All good things end - all bad things too.
Everything is finite. An end is always true.
Like a string cut without a measure
There is no length of guarantee.
How long is only ever answered:
There will be an end.

Tie hard the knots, fray well the edges,
Wrap the candles tighter.
Pull taught the stretch of tether,
Spool the bobbin's last reserve –
There will only ever be one answer:
There is an end.

<u>All words are water</u>

These words are water -

The distillation, precipitation of it all -

The nourishment and punishment

That feeds the forest, grows the seed

Wets the ground of love and faith.

That brings the deluge down, bursts the dam

Washes all of hope away.

Calls in the storm, snuffs out the light

Turns the dust to life,

Washes clean, leaves rivulets like veins in hardened ground.

These words

That drizzle, pour, slake, evaporate and drown

And come again…

This rain

Of letters, sounds, intent:

These words of water.

Written, droplet-stained to sink or slip

Words that fall from page and lip,

From heart and breath and pen

This word. These words. All words.

Like water.

Into the Ether

Like leaves that search for sun,
Roots that yearn for rain,
The tongue that longs to speak –
We reach,
Beacon wide our dreams
In words whispered to the ether,
Tentacled in undersea cables
Across the world
Searching in the dark
For the tessellated human heart.
To twang this web of living
To sing something like a truth
To breathe.
To believe.

Hours

Dandelion heads turn to hours,
Silver over what was so soon sun
Bright.
The minutes breathe out
In silk-parachuted moments -
Dreams and wonders
Set adrift
By a wind
That caresses, gentles,
Lifts away
Into the unknown
All the hours and minutes
Gossamered into longing,
Particled and beautiful.
Remembered.
Forgotten

Stage Four

To Katie, who was hijacked by the Big C on Stage Four

Stage Four.

Like some elevator floor,

Or a platform

At some alternate music fest.

(Some; more; full; fuller;

Fullest. Stage Four.)

Where strangers come to dance

And cocktails gleam with radiation.

Where dreams haze over

And the future is painted white.

Stage Four. Stage Four.

There's a knocking at the door:

Strange floodlit places

And dance moves no-one knows….

Stage Four.

The waking wish of a last encore.

The no more, Stage Four.

The bow, the out -

And To All, goodnight…

A flickering billboard.

Stage Four.

Dark

Once,

On a dark, unmarked Germiston street,

I almost hit a train

Where tracks ran dark across the tarmac

And no level crossing marked the spot.

My bewildered dark-stung brain

Wondered at the moving dark against the darker deep –

Stopped a mere metre away.

Saw the shift of containers; heard the rumbling roar.

Once.

On a dark and winding country lane

I almost hit a deer,

Where a sudden leap of headlights

Dark cotton-wooled in mist,

Etched spindle legs and glistened eye.

Stopped a mere metre away.

Breathed together: hypnotised; mesmerised,

Until it and others melted mist-dark to night.

So it is:

This Dark,

The hand of Fear and Wonder.

A net to catch this human heart,

Between the dark of dread; the dark of dreams.

* Germiston – a town in South Africa

Faith

The unlikely sight of a silvered snail rim
At shoulder height –
The culprit tucked asleep against the dew
Pooled in pearls on a drooping grass head –
Anchored tight in the morning sway.
A small snail – whorls still transparent bright –
And the glass-thin stem of grass,
As if in imagining…
What small ambition drove the climb?
What hope? What optimism?
What pulled the reach to up and up
When all the others played it safe,
Took refuge under broader leaves?
What tiny heart saw the thinnest of trails,
And followed to the furthest edge,
To sip the wind on the highest sail,
To glow in the first of the sun?

What faith –

So small,

To reach that precarious height –

And sleep.

December

Dark December.

Faded friend to bright November,

The last of his kind , sunk to dreariness

Of sodden rain and rain and rain

Where days stutter short,

Cowed by gloomy skies and nights stretch long,

Cat-like and sleek with dark dread.

Small wonder this grip of fear,

Of death that will not end,

Small wonder our fearful staving off -

The lights around the doors,

Log fires, spiced wine.

Wall-eyed pretence that we are merry,

Clinging fast to the memory and faith of Spring.

Hold firm, buy dreams, lock the doors

Count the hours -

Through the long dark of December.

Journey by Train

The spool of track unwinds,

Slips away, suspended in time

Through great gulps of city

And fields – green, brown, puddle-studded.

Cows hunker low beneath the shifting sky.

A horse, stark-drawn sentinel on a hill.

A grove of trees all blown down –

Recumbent, with startled roots, still soil-bound

In wide, upended dinner plates.

The swoosh, breathless

Movement without…

Birds on a string in the sky –

A necklace untied.

Lights

In the early December dark

Traffic ribbons like Christmas lights –

Red and white –

Winding away. Spooling out,

Unreal against the inked-black of unlit fields.

For a moment, I am untethered.

Some binding slips from my heart,

And moth-like, caught in a spell of light,

All is emptied into illusion,

Drawn away from the earth,

The safety of warm spaces

Into the traffic that blinds and binds

With promises of prettiness.

Good will to all…

Such is this veneer of festivity,

With all the glitter and the farce,

And the wide empty spaces

Like ink.

Tenderness and Tears

Faith is so hard to keep

Against the whispers of the world,

The unfurl of the airwaves

The rumours of death and dread.

Fine as spider silk

Though taut and tightly tethered,

Faith is too small a word

Against the enormity of it all.

It sleeps instead in granules –

In seeds, secreted beneath the ground,

In this avenue of trees grown old and strong.

In small words and in forgiveness

In tenderness and tears.

It breathes in every sunrise,

In the turnings of the year.

In all the small and living things

That strive and struggle and grow.

Here. Faith is here.

Small. Unspoken. Here.

The Tractor Shed

The half-light of the tractor shed

Washes over me with sudden unexpectedness -

Real and imagined -

Draws down a memory I thought was done…

If I could go back…

It seems so clear:

The dust motes dancing in sunlight

That leaks through holes in the zinc-plate roof.

The smell of diesel.

The concrete floor scattered with dust and straw.

Was it a ten-gallon drum?

Did you have to move it? Roll it into place?

Was that rope easy to knot, or did it take some time?

If I could go back…

If I could be there

Would you talk to me instead?

Would we play childhood games

On the Massey Ferguson, red and loved -

Dream of driving?

Would you believe in tomorrows,

The possibilities of all to come?

If I could go back

And be there?

Ballad of the Voter

All the poets and all their words

Mean nothing now.

Politicians still lie

While boats of desperation crowd the shores

Of bastions that stay strong, all bricked up in righteousness.

The ballot boxes hang heavy

With hope like candyfloss –

All sugared and insubstantial

Opinions bounce off the chamber walls,

Leer back in buffered contortion.

Lies are laid as truths; promises like dandelions

That come and go and blow away

And nothing changes.

All the words and all the poets

Mean nothing.

Now.

Snow

From where I am

The snow smells of childhood,

Cocoons the world in dreaming –

In the white dust of nostalgia

Like an eiderdown,

The feathers of memory

Falling, falling,

Soft as sighs

That sigh the cold. The bleak.

I wonder

If, where the war is -

Death looks darker against the white,

Colder

For the featherings of snow.

End Game

It's a game of seasons, time and turning

And now the cards are dealt, the dice are rolled:

An end game, perhaps,

Of Anthropocene and done

Where glaciers trickle through our fingers

And storms swallow our paved estates

And greed farms out in super-bugs.

Russian roulette reigns in loaded guns…

What will we say?

The polar bears will be okay –

They hunt beluga now –

And urban foxes thrive on scraps.

Species thought extinct are rediscovered.

Is it the Dacians who disappeared.

Angkor Wat lies empty.

All of GDP will measure nothing

When the game is done,

When our season's seen in passing,

When ivy grows thick on these estates

And thistles mark our way.

When life crawls on,

Then will we say:

`It was the end game that we played.'

Here I Am

All these words are written,

All this ink is stained:

Look at me.

Here I am –

Here is the distillation of me

Laid bare, chiselled to the bone.

Here I am.

These words and all the stanzas gone before,

Some small testimony; some trail –

Here I am,

Fragile as breath,

All the meanings ever etched

In this porcelain hope of permanence –

The dream of some mark left behind.

Some spot; some trace; something.

These words, in a rush of a million words

Whispered, washed away, forgotten,

Like air and rain.

Small nothings. Echoes.

Here I am.

Of Love and Mortality

Then, when we leave and close this door,
Will footprints of this past
Hang like stardust in our hearts
And stir our souls to yearning?
Or will the map be coloured over -
A slate wiped clean, erased
Laid bare for new lines
Of dew and weathering?
Perhaps
It all ends with the leaving,
The clicking of the latch,
The silence in the song.
Perhaps there is no more…

I hope there is a thumbprint,
A small warmth of where you touched me,
A soft seed of believing.

I hope there stays an echo, a calling,

Fireflies along the track.

I hope that we will find the way

Back home.

Identity

Still here, but indistinct

Like the closing of a day,

Like the turning of a page

When all the letters slip away.

A story becomes a history,

The day becomes the dark.

And where am I? Where am I?

Shadow and light; dream and truth:

It's all illusion.

And moth wings flutter in my soul:

Dusty, fragile, chasing fire

Of a candle that burns both ends

And is nothing.

Wings beat against the greenhouse glass.

Gasp. Mouth and spirit searching.

These words, these cyphers

These little marks of pen

Reach to catch, to keep, to hold -

Something –

That, like water in a hand,

Slips away.

Will We Know?

One day will be the last day

And we will drift away into the stuff of dreams

And far imagined spaces

Where all is light and letting go.

Will we know?

The last day.

The last dawn chorus.

The last Spring rain; the last Winter snow.

That last sudden burst of laughter

Like a bubble of breathed believing

Before everything slides towards the sun –

Oh, my friend, do you think we will?

Will we know?

Morning

Up to the hill

Where the sigh of silence

Lifts and falls beneath my ribs;

Tastes the rhythm of my heart in the beat of the track

That opens out in Spring-yellowed breathing

Against a sky cloud-gentled

Into grey - like wings

Of this world that cradles the all of me:

Gently - a small and fragile thing

Light feathered as a fledgling:

Blood and bone and dreaming,

Small tethered to the day

By beat and breath

And silence

Revenge

An eye for an eye

And blinded rage will eat the world

In fire and fear and pain.

Call out your name

And write it on the walls –

Have it all –

For vengeance is mine

And yours and theirs

And in the end

No-one cares, or remembers why it is

That you stand your ground -

Your little patch of earth

That shifts and falls away

All barb-wire rimmed and sullen shelled

And mercy-bare…

This island of your echoes,

Graffitied in your name

Where all who once loved you

Leave.

Follower

Follow me.

This snail trail that gleams silver

Over paths and leaf edges,

The pathos and crescendo,

Soft-bodied in supplication.

Like me.

As if the liking might look to move –

What?

No worlds or weathers –

This ether. This following.

The snail or the piper,

The bird or the rat –

Either way

It ends badly

In bruising and worse –

This false trail, shiny bleed of art.

This fragility of feeling,

This ticking validation.

Just see. Just be.

Get Up

I don't know why I didn't die

When the world shifted -

Hung hopes and dreams from the rafters.

I don't know why

When a heart was cold and wrung

And a brain small-stunned and numb,

When everything and all that was

Bled out in gouts of grief,

When gut-held guilt haggled at the breath,

I don't know why

I didn't die.

Perhaps

It was something in the April air -

The glimmer of light against the horizon,

The opening of the earth towards the sun.

That lesson from the universe:

Get up! Get up!

Life will bloom and song will come –

Get up! Get Up!

There are yet miracles to be had.

The whole world breathes in faith

That day will follow night

And death will follow life

And life

Will win.

<u>Time Heals</u>

The hawthorn berries are out, red

Against the green.

Last year they bled, this year they jewel –

Because time heals all.

A rainbow spans the sky

High-arcing above the stubbled field

And light prisms the dark edge of the woods.

A flock of pigeons wheels,

Wings improbably bright in the rain-scored sun.

The white and light

Flare like joy across the cloud-dark sky,

And berries like rubies

And time heals all.

Falling

Clocks go back –

Arms wide, eyes closed,

Free-fall into darkness,

Become leaves that fall -

Let go and scatter –

Fall away from sun and summer

In yellow:

Fall, fall…

Into deeper places where memory

Pools and pulls

Into winter and turning seasons.

Look back. Fall back,

Eyes closed

With clocks and time

And beating hearts

Falling.

All That We Are

All we have and all we are

And all of what is cast adrift –

Those small satellites of memory that blink –

Tethered to the spiderwebs that streak my hair.

The silences and songs

Mapped in the creases of my face

That catch the rain.

This long living; this long losing.

Who we were and what we dreamed

In those imagined salad days

When all was flame and possibility

The world an oyster filled with rage and righteousness

And hope and fear and love and fear. And fear.

And so the years spill a sort of emptiness.

A letting go; a long surrender

Into the embrace of silence. Acceptance.

The quiet breathing of life and loss

To see the silver in the grey;

Taste the sweetness of the rain.

Memory

The light slants across the table –

This evening sun, this African sun,

Strokes at the candelabra, the chrysanthemums -

The yellow light across the dark wood

As if this were a memory,

The accumulation of family,

The incongruity of the familiar

In the evening African sun:

The slots we slide into.

The moment is spotlit,

Dusty and new.

Suspended. Remembered.

The slow slipping of the day -

The trail of us

In photographs and chrysanthemums.

The Poets and the Dreamers

When the clouds rolled in
And the world grew dark
And the storm of derision came close;
Then all seemed lost.
All gone, all cold, all weak
Against the roar of the incoming tide
Hard and heavy with hate.
But…

But the poets and the dreamers
Stood firm,
The weave of their words like candles
Small
And bright against the night.
And as they said, they lit a way:
A path. A place.
A hope.

Letterbox

Stowed away in the letterbox,

The voice of childhood memory

Paused, like a butterfly pinned

In a moment – gone

But echoed. Alive again

In words written

When we were young

And filled with possibility;

When we wrote of nothing and everything

When we

Lived.

Ghosts

December fills with ghosts:

Long echoes of laughter

And how once it was

When all the world suspended and magic reigned

And we were happy for a day.

December fills with ghosts

That gather 'round the table

Whispering of what has been

And calling back haunts so long forgotten;

Those faces once all unlined and candle-lit -

Now cast in fading photographs

And ghosts.

This Longing

And out there

Just beyond this touch of air

Is All

That calls to this part of me

That has no name

But yearns for what it cannot reach –

That touch of just beyond,

That breath that skims the ear

To call us back, back. Back

To turn to see the empty street,

That brushes the nape of the neck

Like the lips of a lover

Lost. Somewhere

Calls, calls my name

In words that atoms cannot hold.

Tugs

Like the pull of a lifebelt;

A straitjacket; a kite;

A ribbon swirled loose

Where the end is just beyond

The reach of blood and touch.

Just beyond, just there -

Behind this curtain of atmosphere,

This what is.

This longing.

Ordinary things

The spider's web

That gathers the morning dew

And spans silver the space

Between the lavender heads;

These small and ordinary things -

These lanes and fields and muddied ways -

That scribe a breath into words,

That taste of bright edges

And hidden spaces

That roll against my tongue.

These ordinary things

Breathe of sweetness,

Taste of dreams,

Speak in forgotten songs,

Fill and feed,

The empty space of me.

If We Mine The Moon

If we mine the moon

And sell the stars,

If we tunnel into dreams,

Extract rare earths from imagination.

If we mine the moon,

What then the sky goddess,

The pull of blood and ties?

What then the call of wolves,

The lantern in the dark?

If we mine the moon

We will dream of nothing –

Of a void of excavated rock,

Of the end of magic.

If we mine the moon –

Convert our longing into flesh.

What then the stuff of wishing

Become another Thing.

Waiting

It's pin pricks

And pooled blood

And a sort-of pointlessness to it all –

These little rays of living,

Pebble-bright

And hard –

All shape and shadow,

Facetted, reflective,

Saying nothing at all

While beaming back the images.

All ruby-red and glowing.

Stone cold, bled dry

Until all there is,

Is a holding on;

Waiting for the night to turn to dew,

For the dark to be all silvered –

For the chance to blink.

Clockwork

Time stretches endless
In childhood limbs that glow with sun
And while away the ageless days of school
In dreams of Summers that seem so long,
And an hour is the making of a moon.

So soon, the clock escapes the cage
And seconds tick away
Into years
And life
And all that happens in between.
We blink:
Limbs grow old, joints cold,
Moons seem sudden impossibilities
Adrift in a different season.
A blink:
Summer winks to Winter.

Solstice

This, the night of longest dark;

This deepest Winter

When the day has scarce opened in heaviness

And grey

And the scent of Spring seems so far away.

This solstice stretches, wraps like a cloak

Made of wind and bite

And dark; and dark

That muffles quiet and small the spark,

That tiny glowing ember of renewal,

Of tomorrow.

Tomorrow:

When the day will be longer,

The light will be closer –

Minutely -

By the breadth of a hair,

Like the spin of a web

That tugs us closer, closer,

Turning the wheel towards the sun.

Tonight is not so dark, nor so bleak;

Not so heavy now

This heart knows of Tomorrow –

The hope of the day after –

Tomorrow.

When the world will tilt and turn

Into promise.

This heart knows

The night is always deepest

Just before the dawn.

New Year's Eve

Then we tamed the seasons

- Sydney Bridge; London Eye; Times Square –

Declared the year made new

In fireworks and Auld Lang Syne,

In wishes and resolutions and letting go.

All bound to a time, chained to a clock:

The tick, the tock,

The regimented beat of sixty-sixty-twenty-four.

And so we tied forever,

Turned the never to a finite thing.

That rings in the changes, tallies the calendar,

Calibrates the year.

And somewhere far from here –

Where the jungle's deep and the desert's wide -

In places where this night is just the dark

And silent stars turn the sky –

The new day will be just another.

There, time is still untethered

Told in the roll of the Earth,

The toll on the flesh,

In birth and death.

There, time flows like a river

On

Carrying dreaming unfurled:

No endings, no fireworks,

Nothing to hold.

Where history is a memory

And time is told as seasons

These Words

These words are not mine.

They have slipped my blood,

Spilled from my ribs and heart,

Been exhaled

To lie like casing on the page –

Footprints that lead away:

Memories.

You can have them, if you like –

Let them rattle in your pocket like rocks,

Or drop them where the soil is soft,

To grow…

Or roll them on your tongue,

Breathe them out, to float away

Like dandelion seeds

Into the air of dreaming.

Away, away.

From me. From you.

They are not ours.

Mandy lives in Shropshire, England with her husband, youngest daughter and an indefatigable terrier called Skipper.

Her favourite things are books, plants, trees, wild things - and tea.

This is her seventh collection of poetry.

Other works:

<u>*Poetry*</u>

Whispers from Southern Lands (2019)

Evidence (2019)

Fieldsong (2020)

Crow Dancing (2022)

Greening (2023)

Small Breath (2024)

<u>*Novel*</u> *(MJ Whyman)*

Like Water (2022)

www.ingramcontent.com/pod-product-compliance
Lightning Source LLC
Chambersburg PA
CBHW072136070526
44585CB00016B/1706